Summ
of

Own The Day, Own Your Life
Aubrey Marcus

Conversation Starters

By BookHabits

Please Note: This is an unofficial Conversation Starters guide. If you have not yet read the original work, you can <u>purchase the original book here.</u>

Copyright © 2018 by BookHabits. All Rights Reserved. First Published in the United States of America 2018

We hope you enjoy this complementary guide from BookHabits. Our mission is to aid readers and reading groups with quality, thought provoking material to in the discovery and discussions on some of today's favorite books.

Bonus Downloads
Get Free Books with __Any Purchase__ of Conversation Starters!

Every purchase comes with a FREE download!

Add spice to any conversation
Never run out of things to say
Spend time with those you love

Scan Your Phone

Tips for Using Conversation Starters:

EVERY GOOD BOOK CONTAINS A WORLD FAR DEEPER THAN the surface of its pages. Questions herein are designed to bring us beneath the surface of the page and invite us into the world that lives on. These questions can be used to:

- Foster a deeper understanding of the book
- Promote an atmosphere of discussion for groups
- Assist in the study of the book, either individually or corporately
- Explore unseen realms of the book as never seen before

Table of Contents

Introducing *Own The Day, Own Your Life*

O wn the Day, Own Your Life: Optimized Practices for Waking, Working, Learning, Eating, Training, Playing, Sleeping, and Sex is a book written by Aubrey Marcus, a proponent of holistic health philosophy. It teaches readers how to make positive changes in one's life by living optimally in a single day.

The book focuses on what an individual can do in a single day, and how good choices made within the 24-hour period will lead to a life-changing mind and body well-being.

Marcus poses the question of how one day can make a difference and provides answers by outlining guidelines, practical tips, and lots of examples and inspiration from high performing athletes, coaches, thinkers, and other personalities who are outstanding in their own fields. He breaks down aspects of a single day into fitness, nutrition, productivity, mind-set, sex, performance, and sleep and says these are all related to each other. All of these are necessary to live a worthy life and should be optimized in one's daily routine. At the end of the day, one's life is meaningful based on how one feels, with whom one makes connections, and how much fun one had.

Written in a light, casual, friendly and motivational tone, Marcus's book is composed of 16 chapters that help readers focus on every important aspect of their daily life. He starts with a chapter on the importance of water and hydration to start the day. He adds an explanation on why it important to get enough hours of sleep. He shares details about sea salt, circadian rhythm, sunlight, movement, illustrations of exercise moves, water sources, even a story about the philosopher Marcus Aurelius on citing the importance of discipline, all these to highlight the chapter's focus on starting the day energized. Chapter Two focuses on proper breathing and the secrets of the ancients who used breath techniques to energize themselves. Chapter

Three is all about eating the right food and in the right way. The rest of the chapters include: the importance of supplements, the proper use of time, plants as sources of energy, working well, the right and weird way to lunch, power naps, right exercise and training, playtime, dinnertime, better sex, and the right way to sleep. Marcus uses a lot of quotes and stories about people who are exemplary, ancient and contemporary. Many of them are philosophers and great thinkers like Einstein and Neitzche. He quotes Goethe in the introduction to stress the importance of the single day. Among athletes he cites college football coach Nick Saban, whom he consider the greatest in the history of coaching. Along with the great people, he also quotes important books and sources like the samurai master Miyamoto Musashi and his book *Book of Five Rings*. To make reading easy and memorable, ideas and tips are summarized in each chapter. To further make his tips implementable, he gives detailed instructions that could be done right away. The book's conversational tone is even made more appealing with Marcus' humor. His explanations include scientific sources and makes them understandable with simplified yet intelligent language. For example, he explains stress and energy in terms of immune response, and relates these to reproduction, growth, and digestion processes, musculoskeletal efficiency and cognitive performance.

He talks about the stress hormones cortisol, adrenaline, and norepinephrine and how these influence human lives. He cites sources like the Institute of Medicine and National Research Council to point out studies on age, death and survival rates. Apart from the science, he also delves into mythological, historical and ancient practices. In explaining breath techniques, he mentions *Tummo*, the Inner Fire meditation, and the tradition of pranayama or deliberate breath control practiced by yogis. He cites some anthropological research as well. He cites the Powhatan Indians who maintain their health by practicing the tradition of bathing themselves and their babies every single day in the cold waters of Chesapeake Bay. This is supposed to toughen them up. An interesting nontraditional story about plants is recounted in his chapter on the power of plants. He says a Peruvian-trained vegetalista, or plant doctor, told him once that plants are more evolved than humans, and for these to become human beings complicated with emotions and human failures is a step backward in their evolution.

Marcus thinks this is a beautiful metaphor for the importance of plants in human life.

A list of sources and links is provided at the end of the book.

This book is authored by the founder and CEO of Onnit, an organization which promotes Total

Human Optimization based on holistic health philosophy. Its clients include top performing athletes worldwide.

Discussion Questions

"Get Ready to Enter a New World"

Tip: Begin with questions dealing with broader issues to ensure ample time for quality discussions. Read through all discussion questions before engaging.

~~~

question 1

Own the Day, Own Your Life is a book written by Aubrey Marcus, a proponent of holistic health philosophy. What does holistic health philosophy believe in?

~~~

~~~

question 2

The book teaches readers how to make positive changes in one's life by living optimally in a single day. Why does it emphasize the importance of a single day?

~~~

~~~

question 3

The book provides guidelines, practical tips, and lots of examples and inspiration. What kind of people does the author refer to for his examples? What makes these people ideal sources of inspiration?

~~~

~~~

question 4

He breaks down aspects of a single day into fitness, nutrition, productivity, mind-set, sex, performance, and sleep. Why these particular elements?

~~~

~~~

question 5

The book is written in a light, casual, friendly and motivational tone. What is the effect of this kind of tone? How does it make you feel?

~~~

~~~

question 6

The book is composed of 16 chapters that help readers focus on every important aspect of their daily life. How does this structure help you understand the book?

~~~

~~~

question 7

He starts with a chapter on the importance of water and hydration to start the day. Why is it important to do this?

~~~

~~~

question 8

He shares details about sea salt, circadian rhythm, sunlight, movement, illustrations of exercise moves, water sources, even a story about the philosopher Marcus Aurelius on citing the importance of discipline. How does this mix of information help you understand chapter one?

~~~

~~~

question 9

Chapter Two focuses on proper breathing and the secrets of the ancients who used breath techniques to energize themselves. What kind of breathing does Marcus teach and how does one do this?

~~~

~~~

question 10

He quotes Goethe in the introduction to stress the importance of the single day. How does quoting Goethe affect your impression of the book?

~~~

~~~

question 11

He also quotes important books and sources like the samurai master Miyamoto Musashi and his book *Book of Five Rings*. How does his choice of books to cite and quote contribute to the book's content? Do you like his choice of books?

~~~

~~~

question 12

To make reading easy and memorable, ideas and tips are summarized in each chapter. Do you find this helpful? Why? Why not?

~~~

~~~

question 13

To further make his tips implementable, he gives detailed instructions that could be done right away. Have you followed his instructions? What makes them an important part of the book?

~~~

~~~

question 14

The book's conversational tone is even made more appealing with Marcus' humor. Do you like his humor? Why? Why not?

~~~

~~~

question 15

Apart from the science, he also delves into mythological, historical and ancient practices. Which of these practices especially interested you? Why?

~~~

~~~

question 16

Bestselling author Ryan Holiday, says Marcus book gives results that can't be argued with. Why can you not argue against the results?

~~~

~ ~ ~

question 17

Author Shawn Stevenson says the book gives readers the best tools for optimizing your every aspect of your life including body, health, mind. Why do you think these are the best tools?

~ ~ ~

~ ~ ~

question 18

Athlete and bestselling author Lewis Howes says Marcus is the "the Indiana Jones of mind and body optimization." How is he comparable to Indiana Jones?

~ ~ ~

question 19

Jason Feifer of Entrepreneur magazine says the book is ambitious and useful. Why does he call it ambitious?

~~~

question 20

New York Times bestselling author Ben Greenfield says the book is the best guide he has ever read. Do you think it is the best guide you've read so far? Why? Why not?

~~~

Introducing the Author

Aubrey Marcus founded Onnit, an Inc. 500 company that promotes a holistic health program called Total Human Optimization. Marcus has coached top athletes worldwide through his company's programs and products. *Own The Day, Own Your Life* is his first book. His The Aubrey Marcus Podcast engages the leading movers in the fields of science, spirituality, relationships, athletics, and business in enlightening discussions that have been downloaded over 10 million times. Marcus took a degree in philosophy at the University of Richmond. He says he likes philosophy because he likes to solve puzzles involving the mind and body. In his book, he tackles the themes on forgiving ones past mistakes, surrendering to the process instead of the outcome, and using resistance as assistance. Aside from his podcast, he also contributes to *Forbes, Entrepreneur,* The Joe Rogan Experience, and The Doctors. His ideas and tips are also discussed in Go For Your Win, a course he wrote before his current book.

For this Onnit CEO who has appeared on Men's Health cover, Marcus was not always the healthy and optimistic person he is now known for. He was a stressed and depressed person who suffered from blood sugar swings as a result of bad diet. He used to take a lot of toxic substances and was often sick. As his 30th birthday approached, he decided to change for the better. To signify this change, he adopted his middle name Aubrey for his first name. He started making good choices, taking responsibility for his life being the first among them.

He had nothing to guide him through this change so he did a lot of research and talked to people who could give him more information and guidance. He was able to gather tools and practices which helped him create a blueprint for total human optimization. Eventually, his company Onnit was created to help others experience these techniques.

Among of the philosophers he studied in school were the Stoics. He admits that he was able to comprehend and value their teachings only when life became tough for him.

Learning how to respond to life's challenges is something he took from the Stoics.

Though he might not be responsible for the bad things happening in his life, he learned that he is responsible for his response to these difficulties. He could learn to be stronger as a result of life's challenges or he could choose to see himself as a victim.

He says a Stoic attitude teaches that "nothing is really a blessing or a curse."

He quotes on of his favorite philosophers, Epictetus, who says "People are disturbed not by

things, but by the views we take of them."
Another favorite thinker of his is Marcus Aurelius
who he sees is an undeniablyy austeree person.
Aurelius did not like getting out of bed early on
chilly mornings but he did nevertheless. This is
what differentiates high achievers and ordinary
people according to Marcus, they do things they
know are important even if this means it's going to
take an extra effort, or even a huge amount of it. It
is a skill that he teaches in his book.

Fireside Questions

"What would you do?"

Tip: These questions can be a fun exercise as it spurs creativity among the readers by allowing alternate scene endings and "if this was you" questions.

~~~

question 21

Aubrey Marcus founded Onnit, an Inc. 500 company. What is the goal of Onnit?

~~~

~~~

question 22

Marcus took a degree in philosophy at the University of Richmond. What does he like about philosophy?

~~~

~ ~ ~

question 23

Marcus was not always the healthy and optimistic person he is now known for. How was he like before Onnit?

~ ~ ~

~~~

question 24

As his 30th birthday approached, he decided to change for the better. What did he do to mark this change? What attitudes and practices did he adopt?

~~~

~~~

question 25

One of his favorite philosophers is Epictetus. What does Epictetus teach?

~~~

question 26

He breaks down aspects of a single day into fitness, nutrition, productivity, mind-set, sex, performance, and sleep. If you are to add more things to this list, what would that be? Why?

~~~

question 27

Marcus uses a lot of quotes and stories about people who are exemplary, ancient and contemporary. If he limited his references to contemporary personalities, who would you add to the list? What do they teach?

~~~

~~~

question 28

He also quotes important books and sources like the samurai master Miyamoto Musashi and his book *Book of Five Rings*. If you are to add more books to his list, which would you include? Why?

~~~

~ ~ ~

question 29

He also delves into mythological, historical and ancient practices. If you are to rewrite these as lengthier stories in the book, how would you do it?

~ ~ ~

question 30

He talks about the stress hormones cortisol, adrenaline, and norepinephrine and how these influence human lives. If you are to rewrite the science aspect of the book, how would you do it? Why?

Quiz Questions

"Ready to Announce the Winners?"

Tip: Create a leaderboard and track scores to see who gets the most correct answers. Winners required. Prizes optional.

~ ~ ~

quiz question 1

The book teaches readers how to make positive changes in one's life by living optimally in _____day/days

~ ~ ~

~~~

quiz question 2

True or False: At the end of the day, one's life is meaningful based on how one feels, with whom one makes connections, and how much fun one had.

~~~

quiz question 3

He starts with a chapter on the importance of
_____and hydration to start the day.

~~~

quiz question 4

Chapter Two focuses on proper _____ and the secrets of the ancients who used breath techniques to energize themselves.

~~~

~~~

quiz question 5

True or False: He quotes Einstein in the introduction to stress the importance of the single day.

~~~

quiz question 6

True or False: Marcus uses a lot of quotes and stories about people who are exemplary, ancient and contemporary.

~~~

quiz question 7

True or False: In explaining breath techniques, he mentions *Tummo*, the Inner Fire meditation, and the tradition of pranayama or deliberate breath control practiced by yogis.

~~~

~~~

quiz question 8

Aubrey Marcus founded _____, an Inc. 500 company that promotes a holistic health program called Total Human Optimization.

~~~

~~~

quiz question 9

Marcus took a degree in _____ at the
University of Richmond.

~~~

quiz question 10

True or False: Before Onnit, he was a stressed and depressed person who suffered from blood sugar swings as a result of bad diet.

quiz question 11

True or False: : Among of the philosophers he studied in school were the Stoics. He admits that he was able to comprehend and value their teachings only when life became tough for him.

~ ~ ~

quiz question 12

True or False: As his 40th birthday approached, he decided to change for the better. To signify this change, he adopted his middle name Aubrey for his first name.

~~~

Quiz Answers

1. one
2. True
3. water
4. breathing
5. False
6. True
7. True
8. Onnit
9. philosophy
10. True
11. True
12. False

Ways to Continue Your Reading

EVERY month, our team runs through a wide selection of books to pick the best titles for readers and reading groups, and promotes these titles to our thousands of readers – sometimes with free downloads, sale dates, and additional brochures.

[Click here to sign up for these benefits.](#)

If you have not yet read the original work or would like to read it again, you can [purchase the original book here.](#)

On the Next Page...

If you found this book helpful to your discussions and rate it a 4 or 5, please write us a review on the next page.

Any length would be fine but we'd appreciate hearing you more! We'd be very encouraged.

Till next time,

BookHabits

"Loving Books is Actually a Habit"

Made in the USA
Coppell, TX
16 June 2023

18187792R10039